# Table of Contents

# Introduction

The United States has been home to several influential military theorists who changed how the United States and other countries protect national interests, train, equip, and fight wars. Among these theorists are Alfred T. Mahan, Billy Mitchell, and more recently Arthur Cebrowski. Their theories were adopted by the United States government resulting in changes to how the nation organized for its national defense and protected its national interests. Given the scope of potential change that a new military theory can affect, it is important to understand the purpose of the theory, the process by which it advanced through the government and the stakeholders that influence the theory and shape its acceptance by the United States government. For a military officer to advance a military theory through the government and potentially multiple stakeholders, they must move through an informal process to get their theory accepted to create policy. By understanding this process, policymakers and military professionals alike can better identify a military theorist and assist how he/she, can advance a theory to policy. The acceptance of a military theory by the United States government is the transition of a theory to policy.

This informal process is the path less travelled; it requires an alignment of various tangible and intangible components to enable the officer to develop and advocate their theory to the point where the government makes policy. The theorist must have a mentor within the military that recognizes their talent and places them in positions to develop and learn to enable eventual access to policy level of the United States government. The theory the officer develops must be consistent with the foreign policy initiatives of the United States. Once at the policy level of government they must have a patron within the government that can advance the theory to the point of policy. Along the way, the officer may encounter various stakeholders operating at the policy level of government; at that level, the officer must rely on some form of military ethics to ensure they are meeting the needs of the Nation rather than the needs of the theory. The challenges presented above occur while on the path of theory becoming policy, before entering that path the military officer/burgeoning theorist must be educated and then develop a theory for implementation. This education and theory development is through the self-study and intellectual

1

curiosity of each officer. The three officers where neither directed by someone in the military to develop a theory nor did they receive a formal education on how to develop a military theory that supports the interests of the United States. There exists no process to identify and train potential theorists; it is only through the support of mentors, the education and self-study of the theorist, and access to a patron, that an officer can advance a theory.

The process by which the theories of A.T. Mahan, Billy Mitchell, and Arthur Cebrowski were adopted shows an increasingly complex environment with several basic components that remain constant. These components are a mentor within the military to avail the theorist of the opportunities for advancement, a civilian patron within the government willing to support and advance the theory and a broadly defined theory that supports national interests. The evolution of the process is manifest in the increase of many and diverse stakeholders, from the media to think tanks to the defense industry. These potential stakeholders, among others, may cloud the base purpose these theories were devised, to address for the United States the desire to maintain access and influence throughout the world.[1]

When addressing these theorists chronologically, there is increasing involvement of other stakeholders in the process beyond that of merely the theorist and patron in the government. It begins with A.T. Mahan having personal access and influence with such key government figures as Theodore Roosevelt, Senator Henry Cabot Lodge, Secretary of State John Hay, and Elihu Root.[2] A.T. Mahan produced the bulk of his work in the late nineteenth century and early twentieth century. The period following the Civil War was that of expansion for the United States. Where in the United States purchased Alaska from Russia, annexed Hawaii, gained Cuba, Puerto Rico, and the Philippines from Spain because of the Spanish American War, and sent troops to China to defend European colonial

---

[1] United States Army, Field Manual 3-07 *Stability Operations* (Washington, DC: United States Army, 2008), vi.

[2] Warren Zimmermann, *First Great Triumph How Five Americans Made Their Country a World Power* (New York, NY: Farrar, Strauss and Giroux, 2002), 8.

interests in the Boxer Rebellion. A.T. Mahan provided the United States with a theory of sea power that led to the creation of a navy fleet capable of securing the United States' newly-acquired interests throughout the world, particularly the colonial expansion into the Pacific. The theory he developed resonated with the group of expansionist politicians to which he had access. They found Mahan's theory capable of providing their expansionist goals with the intellectual underpinning necessary to gain political acceptance for policies that built the type of navy necessary to sustain an empire. Mahan's theory was incorporated into national policy after the publication of his book, *The Influence of Sea Power upon History, 1660-1783* in 1890.[3]

Billy Mitchell returned from Europe following World War I with the United States the preeminent and yet unacknowledged, global power. During this period, the United States was in a period of great technological growth, consumerism, and social change known as the "Roaring Twenties." The United States also confronted the lingering effects from the carnage of World War I and its resulting disillusionment.

Billy Mitchell did not have the same level of success as A.T. Mahan with patrons in the government. He did, however, maintain influence among a cadre of Senators like James W. Wadsworth Jr. (R-New York) and Congressmen such as Charles Curry (R-California), Frank Reid (R-Illinois), and Fiorella LaGuardia (R-New York). These relationships were due to Mitchell living, albeit tenuously, in the same social strata as these politicians as well as being the son of former Senator John Lendrum Mitchell. Additionally, Billy Mitchell constantly published magazine articles to advocate for airpower. He did this to support his overextended lifestyle and to further his personal crusade for airpower.[4] His

---

[3] A.T Mahan, *The Influence of Sea Power upon History, 1660-1783* (Boston, MA: Little, Brown and Company, 1890).

[4] James Cooke, *Billy Mitchell* (Boulder, CO: Lynne Rienner Publishers, 2002), 111, 161.

writings not only increased his popularity with the American public but also made them informed stakeholders in military policy decisions.

Mitchell advocated for his theory of airpower either through his personal relationships or in his position as a senior military officer on the Army staff. His position required him to testify before Congressional committees. Regardless of these efforts, Mitchell's theory never took root during his lifetime, as his theory of air power was neither considered the best means to secure national interests nor was he able to secure the appropriate patronage necessary to advance the theory. Mitchell's ideas concerning airpower, a national air force, and department of defense did come to fruition because of shifting national interests, but only after World War II and the eventual rise of the Soviet threat. [5]

This lesson of military theory being accepted is present again with the work of Arthur Cebrowski. His theory centers on the examples provided by the business successes from using information technology in the late 1980s and early 1990s. The economic gains from the rapid leveraging of information technology were considered comparable to potential military gains. His theory found great support within the George W. Bush administration because it supported their strategy for transforming and using the military across the globe as seen through the "functioning core" and "non-integrated gap" environment envisioned by Cebrowski's then colleague at the Naval War College, military theorist Thomas P.M. Barnett. [6]

Barnett divided the world map into two areas, a functioning core and a non-integrated gap. The functioning core is those parts of the world that are actively integrating their national economies into a global economy and that adhere to globalization's emerging security rule set. The non-integrated gap

---

[5] Billy Mitchell, "Winged Defense." In *Roots of Strategy Book 4*, ed. David Jabolonsky (Mechanicsburg, PA: Stackpole Book, 1999), 430.

[6] James R. Blaker, *Transforming Military Force The Legacy of Arthur Cebrowski and Network Centric Warfare* (Westport, CT: Praeger Security International, 2007), 210.

4

consists of regions of the world that are largely disconnected from the global economy and the rule sets that define its stability.[7]

Cebrowski's efforts to advance his theory were bolstered by the input of stakeholders from think tanks and the defense industry. *A Project for the New American Century* was a think tank made up of prominent conservative thinkers like Donald Kagan and Thomas Donnelly, as well as executives from defense manufacturers like Northup Grumman Corporation and System Planning Corporation.[8] *A Project for the New American Century* published a paper focusing on strategic and military planning priorities for the incoming Presidential administration of 2001. This paper, *Rebuilding America's Defenses Strategy, Forces and Resources for a New Century,* provided the foundation for many of the early defense initiatives of the George W. Bush administration. The key finding, as it relates to Cebrowski's theory, of the paper was that:

> There must be increased funding for military modernization and transformation to meet the United States defense requirements. If funding does not increase for modernization and transformation, there will be a lessened capacity for American global leadership and, ultimately, the loss of a global security order that is uniquely friendly to American principles and prosperity.[9]

This policy, as presented by *A Project for the New American Century,* appears to be supporting the realist theory of American foreign policy, which was popular with government officials at the time. This realist theory is the belief that interests and the quest for power in international relations rather than

---

[7] Thomas Barnett, *The Pentagon's New Map* (New York, NY: JP Putnam Son's, 2004) A collection of rules (both formal and informal) that delineates how some activity normally unfolds. *The Pentagon's New Map* explores the new rule sets concerning conflict and violence in international affairs—or under what conditions governments decide it makes sense to switch from the rule set that defines peace to the rule set that defines war.

[8] Thomas Donnelly, *Rebuilding America's Defenses Strategy, Forces and Resources For a New Century* (Washington, DC: The Project for the New American Century, 2000). http://www.newamericancentury.org/RebuildingAmericasDefenses.pdf (accessed May 8, 2009)

[9] Ibid., v, 90.

5

ideals and benevolence drive countries.[10] The focus on transformation and modernization dove-tales

perfectly with the military theory of Arthur Cebrowski and provides a strong foundation for the theory's

acceptance by the United States government.

This type of stakeholder involvement, through a think tank and the defense industry, causes

government policymakers to question the purpose of these outside groups and to determine whether their

input does in fact improve the quality of the debate about a military theory in question. In this particular

case, the military theorist and the think tank used the same language and advocated for the same changes.

A think tank may want to engage by providing careful study and reflection on the subject, thereby

raising the level of discourse or it may be a single-issue organization funded by defense corporations.

The defense industry has an interest in new military theory because it generally involves the need for new

equipment. Whether battleships, airplanes or computer hardware, new theories can generate new force

requirements and provides profit potential for interested stakeholders. The pursuit of new equipment

based on the requirements developed from a military theory, however, should be approached with

caution. U.S. force development should be driven by how the forces might be employed to protect

national interests. Prior to 9/11, "capabilities-based" defense analysis reinforced shallow thinking about

war and disconnected war from policy and strategy. The focus on capabilities elevated a desired military

capability to that of strategy or policy.[11] In the case of Billy Mitchell, his theory of air power was applied

during World War II with the less than expected results. The beliefs that the bomber will always get

through, and that anti-aircraft artillery would be ineffective, proved to be false. In the European theater,

---

[10] Walter Russell Mead, *Special Providence American Foreign Policy and How It Changed the World*, (New York, NY: Routledge, 2002), 34.

[11] H.R. McMaster, "Learning from Contemporary Conflicts to Prepare for Future War," *Orbis 52* (Fall 2008), http://www.fpri.org/enotes/200810 mcmaster.contemporaryconflictsfuturewar.html (accessed September 8, 2009)

the United States lost 18,000 planes with the majority of those losses due to ground fire.[12] The central

place that the technology held in Mitchell's theory of air power did not consider the potential of other

technology, i.e. anti-aircraft guns, to effect the application of the theory.

To develop a foundation for future analysis of the roles and purposes of the stakeholders in

military theory and the theory's relationship to national policy, several areas must be explained and their

linkages among them shown. Military theory and its role in the United States will be explained using

both Clausewitz and Jomini with their respective definitions of military theory. Clausewitz's idea of the

trinity and the linkage of war and policy, and Jomini's concept of theory that directs action, will frame the

United States' understanding of the role of military theory. National policy as it relates to military theory

will focus on United States foreign policy. A review of the traditions of foreign policy will provide the

context in which military theory must operate as these traditions interact to determine national interests.

Once an understanding of the how and why of military theory is developed, this paper will transition to

review of the actual process through which military theory goes to become policy. To begin this

transition, an overview of professional military ethics demonstrates how professional responsibility and

the expected role of military officers shape the process by which each military theory becomes policy.

Policymaking and stakeholders will be addressed to set the context in which each theorist operated and

the challenges they faced as they moved their theory forward. The determination of the role of

stakeholders in developing and implementing military theory will focus primarily on government

policymakers, think tanks, and the defense industry.

Case studies of A.T. Mahan, Billy Mitchell, and Arthur Cebrowski will illustrate the process by

which a military theory is adopted by the United States government, primarily through patrons and how

---

[12] *The United States Strategic Bombing Surveys. Summary Report (European War)*,
http://www.ibiblio.net/hyperwar/AAF/USSBS/ETO-Summary html, (accessed March 29, 2010), Kenneth Werrell,
*Archie, Flak, AAA, and SAM*
http://www.dtic.mil/cgibin/GetTRDoc?AD=ADA421867&Location=U2&doc=GetTRDoc.pdf (accessed March 29,
2010)

these theories supported national interests. With the review of these various and competing interests, the foundation necessary for analysis will become clear. The process by which a military theory is accepted and applied in the United States is one of a confluence of stakeholders, interests, national policy, and military capability.[13] To accommodate these numerous interests and advance a military theory requires several components from the theory, the theorist, and the patron. When these components align, a military theory is able to move through the United States government to become policy.

## Role of Military Theory in Supporting National Policy

The romanticized idea of a brilliant, career military officer developing military theory and recording it for posterity, or for the betterment of their fellow officers, is not typically reality. For military theory to be adopted to form policy, it cannot be immune to neither the circumstances of the time nor the politics of the day. The theorist must be aware of the world of politics and of stakeholders in and out of the government. With this awareness, the theorist can more successfully link their theory to the politics that govern the making of policy and strategy. Military theory resides in a difficult area between the complexities of governance and the conduct of war. Navigating between war and peace requires clarity as to the purpose of military theory. The purpose of military theory has evolved from its role as defined by German theorist, Carl von Clausewitz as a tool to understand war to its current examples to where theory provides a policy or plan of action.

Carl von Clausewitz most famously articulated the inextricable linking of war and politics in his seminal work, *On War.*[14] Since its publication in 1832, it has become a touchstone for any discussion about theory, war, politics and strategy. Clausewitz argues that the first part of understanding a theory of

---

[13] Charles Lindblom and Edward Woodhouse, *The Policy-Making Process, Third Edition*, (Upper Saddle River, NJ: Prentice Hall, 1993), 11. Policymaking is, instead, a completely interactive process without beginning or end.

[14] Carl von Clausewitz, *On War*, trans. Michael Howard and Peter Paret (Princeton, NJ: Princeton University Press, 1976)

8

war is not to view war as something autonomous, but always as an instrument of policy. By linking war and policy, one can understand the nature, motives and character of war. War is more than a chameleon that slightly adapts to the given case; rather, it is a total phenomenon with dominant tendencies that exist as a paradoxical trinity. The trinity consists of passion and enmity, chance and creativity, and policy. The trinity is the people (passion and enmity) commander and his army (chance and creativity) and the government (policy).

When war occurs, these three tendencies constantly interact with each other in unpredictable ways. The task therefore is to develop a theory that maintains a balance between these tendencies, like an object suspended between three magnets. The purpose of finding the balance point among these three magnets is to develop a theory that can analyze the constituent elements of war, explain in full the properties of the means employed and their probable effects, define clearly the nature of the ends, and illuminate all phases of warfare through critical inquiry. In Clausewitz's view, theory is a guide to anyone who wants to learn about war from books; the theory will light their way, ease progress, train judgment, and help avoid pitfalls. [15] This definition of theory, however, limits it to the realm of the study of war and politics, not to a plan of action. Expanding this definition was Antoine Henri Jomini, the other preeminent military theorist of the nineteenth century.

In his 1838, work *The Art of War*, Jomini presented that military theory, if founded in the right principles, sustained by actual events of wars, and added to accurate history, will form a true school of instruction. Jomini based the theory upon a small number of fundamental principles whose application will almost assure success. His definition of military theory moved it decisively away from the academic endeavor of understanding to the more practical realm of application. This shift in meaning did not completely forgo the key concepts of military theory presented by Clausewitz. The concept of the

---

[15]Ibid., 88,89, 141; For more on the trinity see; Book 1, Chapter 1, sections 27-28.

unpredictability of the elements of the trinity are captured in Jomini's description of war as a drama with a thousand physical and moral causes that operate more or less powerfully and cannot be reduced to mathematical calculations.[16]

Jomini also recognizes the necessary link between war, policy and the government. While Clausewitz sees the link between war and government as a complex and evolving relationship where all elements of trinity will exert influence on the course of the war, Jomini sees the role of government in war as a far more static relationship. The government concludes whether a war is proper, opportune, or indispensable, and determines the various operations necessary to attain the object of the war. Once the government makes this determination, the general is free to conduct the determined course as they see fit. As Jomini contends, a general whose genius and hands are tied by an Aulic council, five hundred miles distant, cannot be a match for one who has liberty of action, other things being equal.[17]

Both Clausewitz and Jomini remain influential theorists throughout the United States military and because of this influence, it is important to acknowledge their differences as to the definition of military theory. Clausewitz applies military theory as a tool for learning and understanding while Jomini applies it as tool for action. The United States military may litter its doctrine with quotes from Clausewitz, but its theories, on the contrary, they take a distinctly Jominian bent. Whether it is Mahan's six elements of sea power or Cebrowski's nine principles of Network-centric Warfare, the dominant belief in the United States of what makes up military theory is that it contains small number fundamental principles to direct action. Mahan, Mitchell and Cebrowski all provide theories for action.

The actions these three military theories present are to support the government and its national policy. By producing theories that advocate action, the theorist or their patron must recognize multiple

---

[16] Antoine Henri Jomini, "The Art of War," in *Roots of Strategy Book 2*, ed. J.D. Hittle (Harrisburg, PA: Stackpole Books, 1997), 437, 556.

[17] Ibid., 449.

stakeholders. The determination of national policy, and the military theory to support it, requires input from numerous stakeholders. The stakeholders required all reside somewhere within the sides of Clausewitz's trinity. They all interact in unpredictable ways and thus, the theory must remain balanced among the three while simultaneously taking action. This task requires a clear understanding of what role the United States government expects its military theory to perform and productive relationships with the necessary stakeholders. The role of military theory in the United States is one of projection outside the nation's borders. The United States military's role is to protect the nation. It does not have compelling internal security concerns and it is geographically isolated from other world powers. This internal stability and isolation has allowed the United States to reach out globally, primarily through commerce, to enhance its world standing and security. This external focus shapes how military theory supports United States policy, and specifically its foreign policy.

## United States Foreign Policy

United States military theory must closely support its foreign policy. This is the case because the military protects national interests made manifest through stated foreign policy. Regardless of the particulars of policy concerning individual countries or regions, the United States has three national interests that have remained unchanged since the nation's founding. The first interest is physical protection, the protection from attack of its territory, people, and their property and the preservation against external threats of its domestic political system and structure of civil values. Second, Americans will expect their government to see to their nation's, and their own economic prosperity, to promote the domestic welfare. Third, Americans will probably continue to insist, as they have since Revolutionary times, that their government attune its foreign policies to the values for which they believe their country stands. [18]

With these three national interests in mind, the United States has developed various methods and traditions of foreign policy to address these national interests. For analyzing the role of military theory in the context of foreign policy traditions, the works of Walter McDougall and Walter Russell Mead will provide the framework to understanding the role military theory in foreign policy. McDougall provides a broader view of foreign policy than does Mead as the former provides the broader purpose of foreign policy over time while the latter provides tasks that must be accomplished to achieve the purpose of foreign policy.

Walter McDougall's *Promised Land, Crusader State*, is a historical review of United States foreign policy traditions since the country's founding. [19] United States foreign policy is broken down into eight specific traditions that evolved chronologically from 1776 to the 1990s. The first four traditions McDougall defines is labeled as the Old Testament and it took place from 1776 to 1898. The first tradition was to ensure the United States remained free and independent, which leads to the second tradition, unilateral foreign policy, to the third tradition, the promotion of an American system of states, which led to fourth tradition of preventing European influence on the continent and later the hemisphere.

The next block of time of the four traditions from 1898 to present day is labeled the New Testament, and it shows the change in United States foreign policy by its movement towards more preemptive intervention in foreign affairs to shape other societies, to make other countries better by introducing market economies, American ideas of governance, and social programs. These concepts, described as meliorist, first found root in the work of Woodrow Wilson and later reappeared during the

---

[18] Terry Deibel "Strategies before Containment: Patterns for the Future," *International Security 16* (Spring 1992): 82.

[19] Walter McDougall, *Promised Land, Crusader State*, (New York, NY: Houghton Mifflin Company, 1997)

12

Cold War with United States intervention in Vietnam. Vietnam was the first war in which the United States dispatched its military forces overseas, not for the purpose of winning, but to buy time for the war to be won by civilian social programs.[20]

Walter Russell Mead identifies United States foreign policy initiatives through only four schools of thought. These dominant schools are Hamiltonian, Jeffersonian, Jacksonian, and Transcendentalist. All four schools of thought have competed for primacy in the realm of United States foreign policy at one time or another. According to Mead, the Hamiltonian vision has been the most consistently influential of the four schools with respect to the conduct of American foreign policy with its determination of national interests by the commercial interests of the United States.[21] This does not mean that Hamiltonians ignore national defense and other issues but instead it means they arrive at their understanding through the lens of the commercial and economic interests of the United States.[22]

The chief concerns of a Hamiltonian thinker are first, freedom of the seas, the freedom of American citizens, American goods, and American ships to travel wherever they wish in the world in the interests of peaceful trade.[23]American history is full of examples of the United States ensuring freedom of the seas from the Quasi-War with France in 1798 to confronting Somali pirates in 2009. The freedom of the seas remains a paramount concern of the United States. This long history of freedom of the seas has expanded to include a concept of the freedom of the skies. The primacy of freedom of travel by land and sea is a based on the geography of the United States and its settlement and expansion. United States

---

[20] Ibid., 189.

[21] Walter Russell Mead "Hamilton's Way," *World Policy Journal 13*, (Fall 1996): 90; These schools of thought can be reduced to a phrase, Hamiltonians are ultimately concerned with national interests, Jeffersonians with representative democracy, Jacksonians with popular sovereignty, and Transcendentalists with justice.

[22] Ibid., 94.

[23] Walter Russell Mead, *Special Providence,* 106.

people and goods must be able to move quickly across the globe to meet the commercial and economic interests of the United States.

The second concern of a Hamiltonian foreign policy is ensuring places where American sell goods. American diplomacy has consistently concerned itself with opening markets ever since the Revolutionary War. American cargoes must have the same rights and privileges as the cargoes of other nations at the harbors for which they are bound. The final component of this Hamiltonian school of thoughts is the free flow money, not just goods, among trading partners. Governments must, for example, engage in sound fiscal and monetary policies if their currencies are to be useful mediums for international transactions. Hamiltonians argue that American commercial interests provide justification for interventions abroad. [24] Across these world markets, the United States gives special focus to regions that possess materials of military significance and energy interests such as when the United States government sponsored military interventions throughout Central and South America to foster the growth of the Mexican oil industry of the early twentieth century.

For the United States to provide military support to meet these foreign policy objectives, it must ground its military strategy in theories that are carefully attuned to enduring tenets of freedom of travel and commerce that have historically shaped foreign policy. All three theorists demonstrate a clear link to the enduring tenets of commerce that govern Hamiltonian foreign policy. The link between theory and policy helped the government to accept the theories, and in turn develop policy to support national interests.

The combination of McDougall's traditions and Mead's four schools of thought provide the context of the foreign policy environment in which the three theorists were operating. This foreign policy environment influenced how the military theories were accepted, and in the cases of A.T Mahan and

---

[24] Ibid., 107, 110, 193.

14

Arthur Cebrowski, matched with the tradition of foreign policy in their time. Mahan's theory supported the progressive imperialism of the late nineteenth early twentieth century by providing a navy with a sustainable global reach while Cebrowski's theory of Network-centric Warfare was consistent with global meliorism, providing a theory of war that could minimize non-combatant causalities and help bring the benefits of globalization to other countries. Billy Mitchell was not successful in advancing his theory of air power during his lifetime for various reasons, one of which was its incompatibility with the foreign policy of his time. Billy Mitchell advocated for air power as a necessary step to defend the United States homeland against the threats of airplanes. America's geographic isolationism and liberal internationalism prevented Mitchell's views on potential air threats, either European or Asian, from gaining the traction necessary to become policy.[25]

When considering the military theories against the Hamiltonian school, they all are postured to support the economic focus demanded by the Hamiltonian school. Each theory provides a means to influence physical locations that generate commerce. From shipping lanes, ports, airports, air routes, etc, each theory provides a means to reach into the commerce-generating centers across the globe. The primary difference in this regard, is in the tools or means to reach out, Mahan provided battleships and coaling stations, Mitchell, airplanes and airfields, and Cebrowski, information technology and persistent surveillance. All three theorists provided a degree of protection of the Hamiltonian school tenets using the great technological advances of their time.

## The Role of the Theorist in Policy Making

The role of the military officer in civil-military relations has been a subject of debate from the time of George Washington and the Continental Army to today. There exists no definitive

---

[25] McDougall, *Promised Land,* The applicable traditions defined by McDougall will receive further explanation in the case studies of each theorist.

answer of what comprises the ideal relationship between civilian and military leaders at the highest levels of government. Rather than wade into that debate, some norms and expectations of behavior for the military theorist will be the focus.

The military theorist operates as part of the broader national security community comprised of civilian and military personnel, as well other actors such as journalists and academics, who contribute intellectual capital and foster debate, legislative bodies with constitutional responsibilities to oversee and provide resources for national security policy, and, finally, the public at large.[26] Given this large number of stakeholders, it has become imperative for the military theorist to be a collaborative member of a team in policymaking. Because of the changes in the process of military theory becoming policy, a collaborative approach is now a key component. Such collaboration did not exist in the times of A.T. Mahan and Billy Mitchell. A.T. Mahan's work went straight to key patrons in the government who could direct policy, like Theodore Roosevelt, Senator Henry Cabot Lodge, Secretary of State John Hay, and Elihu Root.[27] Billy Mitchell had similar access to patrons but was unable to collaborate with these them to a degree necessary to get his theory accepted and adopted as policy. Arthur Cebrowski, however, used a collaborative approach with and through many patrons within the government. His work also naturally coalesced with the work of a think tank highly regarded by the then-current Presidential administration. The ability to collaborate within and among these various stakeholders is politics at the most basic level. The idea of a military officer "playing politics," however, is not generally considered professional ethical behavior.

The role of a military officer in a democratic government has limits of scope and influence. Again, just as in civil-military relations, there is not universal definition of the ethics that govern a

---

[26] Marybeth Peterson Ulrich, "Infusing Normative Civil-Military Relations Principles in the Officer Corps," in *The Future of the Army Profession*, ed. Lloyd Matthews, (Boston, MA: McGraw Hill Company, 2005), 656.

[27] Zimmermann, *First Great Triumph*, 8.

military officer working in a democratic government but Anthony Hartle, former chairman of the English Department at United States Military Academy West Point, has codified seven ethical principles as presented in his book *Moral Issues in Military Decision Making*:

> 1. Accept service to country as their primary duty and defense of the Constitution of the United States as their calling. They subordinate their personal interests to the requirements of their professional functions.
> 2. Conduct themselves at all times as persons of honor whose integrity, loyalty, and courage are exemplary.
> 3. Develop and maintain the highest possible level of professional knowledge and skill.
> 4. Take full responsibility for their actions and orders.
> 5. Promote and safeguard, within the context of mission accomplishment, the welfare of their subordinates as persons, no merely as soldiers, sailors, or airmen.
> 6. Conform strictly to the principle that subordinates the military to civilian authority. They do not involve themselves or their subordinates in domestic politics beyond the exercise of basic civil rights.
> 7. Adhere to the laws of war and the regulations of their service in performing their professional functions.[28]

This list is not the final word on ethical principles, rather it is a compilation of ideas that govern the behavior of military officers. Of particular note is the requirement to subordinate personal interests and ensure the subordination of the military to the civilian leadership. This is consistent with the views of the pre-eminent civil-military relations theorists such as Samuel Huntington, Morris Janowitz, Peter Feaver, Eliot Cohen, etc. Given these ethical principles, it is incumbent on the military theorist, the mentor, and patron alike to understand and ensure the application of the ethics that govern military officers' conduct.

There are several reasons for the limited number of prominent military theorists who are also serving officers. One of the limiting factors is the constraints military ethics place on officers and their input into political debates that ultimately determine policy. This becomes particularly problematic in the realm of military theory. It seems logical that the best theorists and advocates of military theory would

---

[28] Anthony Hartle, *Moral Issues in Military Decision Making*, (Lawrence, KS: University Press of Kansas, 2004), 170.

reside in the military. This has not historically been the case; the military is not a dominant feature at the level of government where theory is made policy. They must constrain their actions within the ethical principles; they simply do not have the same latitude to influence government policymakers as other stakeholders do. The risk military officers' face is in their desire to advance their theory they can overlook those principles for what they determine to be the greater good. Billy Mitchell in his pursuit of his theory, what he determined to be the greater good of the nation, resulted in his Courts-Martial. A Courts-Marital is the most overt result of an ethical lapse, but it can take many subtler forms, through relationships officers form, to meetings they attend, to information they share among other stakeholders, etc. These ethical concerns do not remove the requirement for a military officer to have a patron in the government to advance their theory. These concerns merely add a layer of complexity for the theorist, with only their understanding and application military ethics as their guide through the policy level of government and among the stakeholders in and around the government.

## Key Stakeholders

The key stakeholders in the world of the military theorist are those who work in the defense industry and those in think tanks. Other stakeholders have bearing in the process of the acceptance of military theory and its incorporation into policy, such as journalists, academics, and legislative bodies are some of the major stakeholders. These other stakeholders influence the process but the defense industry and think tanks can challenge the theory directly by virtue of their purported expertise in military affairs.

In its original form, a think tank is a non-profit non-partisan organization engaged in the study of public policy. They perform the following functions (1) carry out basic research on policy problems and policy solutions (2) provide advice on immediate policy concerns that are being considered by government officials (3) evaluate government programs (4) serve as facilitators of issue networks and the exchange of ideas (5) serve as a repository of policy-oriented expertise, for politicians and policy-makers who are out of power. Currently there are over 300 think tanks in the United States, a number

18

which rises to 1300 when university affiliated think tanks are included.[29] Nothing, however, prevents a think tank from being for profit or partisan. Political leaning or monetary gain can and usually shapes the outputs of the five primary functions a think tank performs.

These organizations shape policy not only through the research they provide to policymakers but by serving as a stopover point for policy experts and politicians. They provide these experts for the government, the proverbial bench from which the government can call players into the game. This positioning ensures that they remain in tune with the politics governing policymaking.

A think tank can directly challenge a military theory with a counter theory or they can bolster a military theorist's work with a complementary study, as was the case with Arthur Cebrowski and the think tank, *A Project For the New American Century*. A military theorist has little advantage against such a group. The military theorist has military ethics to ensure the subordinate role of the military to civilian authority. If a think tank provides a contrary view to a civilian policymaker, there is no official means to counter that input. The civilian leadership determines the policy.

Another group of stakeholders is the defense industry, which by virtue of being business enjoys more consideration in the development of policy than would an average citizen group. In the case of the defense industry, it reserves a special position in policymaking decisions because of its role in the economy and national defense. One of the three unchanging national interests is that Americans will expect their government to see to is their nation's and their own economic prosperity, and to promote the domestic welfare.[30] The leadership role that business has in the economy gives executives of large corporations an unusual kind and degree of influence over governmental policymaking. This influence is because of the importance of businesses in meeting one of the nation's primary interests. For the

---

[29] Donald Abelson, Evert Linquist, "Think Tanks in North America," *Think Tanks and Civil Societies*, eds. James McGann, R. Kent Weaver, (New Brunswick, NJ: Transactions Publishers, 2002), 7, 38.

[30] Deibel, "Strategies before Containment," 82.

19

government to try to shape the meeting of this interest, the government offers inducements to businesses in the form of relief from taxes to locate a business in a certain area, favorable banking regulations, among others. Businesses perform their functions well only when governments develop supporting policies that induce investments, assist with aggressive marketing of exports, and otherwise promote a business climate conducive to profitable activities.[31]

This is both a boon and a danger for the United States, a boon in that by creating the proper inducements the United States can reap the economic benefits of the some of the most powerful corporations in world and a danger when several of these industries unite against a policy. Environmental protection is an area of government policy that has at times faced a unified corporate position able to determine policy. This boon and danger argument is also seen in the defense industry, the danger is presented as three-hundred dollar toilet seats, and the boon is having generational advantage in military technology over our adversaries. The defense industry, unlike most large corporations, is in much more of a partnership position with the government.

The defense industry is in a more privileged position than are most large corporations. This is due to the defense industry's role in meeting two of the three enduring national interests, economic prosperity and physical protection against external threats.[32] The relationship between the government, primarily the Department of Defense, and the defense industry is a partnership. The Department of Defense defines this partnership as the Defense Industrial Base. Consisting of the Department of Defense, a large private sector, worldwide industrial complex with capabilities to provide professional services, perform research and development, produce, deliver, and maintain Defense systems,

---

[31] Lindblom, Woodhouse, *The Policy-Making Process*, 91, 92.

[32] Deibel, "Strategies before Containment," 82.

20

subsystems, or components to meet military requirements necessary to fulfill the National Military Strategy.[33]

This partnership encompasses all defense matters concerning the United States. The role of the defense industry executive in policy expends even so far as to shape an independent review of the Congressionally mandated Quadrennial Defense Review. Congress created the 20-member panel in 2006 to analyze the Defense Department's four-year plan, known as the Quadrennial Defense Review. Lawmakers called for the committee to provide an independent "alternate view" of the Pentagon's plan, which shapes future military policy and spending on weapons and other needs. Of this twenty-member panel, eleven work for defense contractors as employees, consultants or board directors.[34] The presence of defense executives on the review panel further demonstrates the influence businesses have in policymaking. As dealing with think tanks, a military theorist can only reach as far as patrons and mentors have access within the defense industry. A military theorist is not free to lobby civilians and advocate their theory, however, as a line exists where the elected officials take information provided and the military officer remains subordinate.

The realm of policymaking is not a level playing field. Those with most influence and access tend to be those groups with the greatest stake in the economy. Just as in the world of foreign policy, economics play a prominent role in policymaking. A military theorist does not make policy; they merely provide information, advice, and recommendations to civilian policy makers. By casting a military theorist in this role, they may be unable to influence the transition of military theory to policy. The value of this military input may be lost and other competing interests have an opportunity to take hold.

---

[33] Ken Krieg, *Defense Acquisition Transformation: Report to Congress*, (Washington: U.S. Department of Defense, 2007) http://www.dtic mil/cgi-bin/GetTRDoc?AD=ADA469464&Location=U2&doc=GetTRDoc.pdf, accessed (March 3, 2010)

[34] Ray Locker, Ken Dilanian, Pentagon Panel has Contractor Contacts, *USA Today*, March 1, 2005, national edition. http://www.usatoday.com/news/military/2010-03-01-pentagon_N.htm, accessed (March 1, 2010)

A.T. Mahan, Billy Mitchell, and Arthur Cebrowski theories were able to advance their theory to implement policy. The path to policy for all three theorists shares some similarities that contributed to their success. A.T Mahan and Billy Mitchell operated in a government that still relied heavily on patronage while moving towards a more professionalized civil-servant workforce. In the case of Arthur Cebrowski, patronage still played a role, but the focus tended to be more on collaboration and limited government.[35]

## A.T. Mahan

Alfred Thayer Mahan was the son of prominent West Point professor Dennis Hart Mahan. He grew up at West Point before eventually going to Annapolis and earning his commission. From there Mahan embarked on a rather pedestrian career as a naval officer. He saw service on blockade duty during the Civil War with a brief interlude of eight months to teach at the Naval Academy, which was then located at Newport, Rhode Island, where he served as the executive officer to then Lieutenant Commander Stephen B. Luce on the Academy's summer cruise to Europe. This chance encounter with Luce was to be instrumental in the shaping his future.[36]

Following his cruise, A.T. Mahan returned to blockade duty and continued his career, with few highlights. In 1875, he was assigned to the Boston Navy Yard, which at the time was being used as an outlet for political patronage and graft. He saw this corruption and through his close friend and prominent North Carolinian, Samuel Ashe, he was able to gain contact with and report these concerns to Senator Merriman of North Carolina. These efforts provided him the opportunity to testify to Congress and that then caused him to be placed on furlough with half pay. The work furlough included numerous officers, and not just Mahan, as it was part of the Secretary of Navy's response to budgetary constraints. This

---

[35] Donald Kilinger, Dahlia Lynn, Beyond Civil Service the Politics of Emergent Paradigms, *Handbook of Human Resource Management in Government, 2nd Ed.*, eds. Stephen Condrey, James Perry (San Francisco, CA: Jossey-Bass Books, 2005), 45.

[36] Zimmermann, *First Great Triumph*, 107.

episode only lasted for three months, but it created a sense of uncertainty about the viability of his naval career. This sense of uncertainty contributed to his desire to publish for money. His first paid publication was in 1878.[37]

As he continued his career, primarily sea duty, he always took extended shore leave. His varied experiences from his extensive travels proved indispensible in his future work. Virtually everything he wrote about the American Navy and naval strategy was based on personal observations. He could advocate for naval reform because he sailed on the obsolete ships and faced corruption at the Navy yards.[38] The opportunity to use these experiences came in 1885 when now-Commodore Stephen Luce asked him to teach strategy, tactics and naval history at the newly formed Naval War College in Newport, Rhode Island. Luce granted A.T. Mahan a year to prepare his lectures; he spent that year in the libraries of New York City. In 1886, A.T. Mahan arrived at Newport and was quickly made acting President of the school as Luce was promoted and reassigned.[39]

Another fortuitous encounter for A.T. Mahan occurred in 1887, when a guest lecturer came to the Naval War College to speak about naval operations during The War of 1812. That lecturer was Theodore Roosevelt. From that encounter, the two men formed a relationship with the shared passion of naval history and the belief that the United States needed to expand its Navy.[40] With his placement at the War College, his new-found relationship with up and coming Republican Theodore Roosevelt, and the continued support of Luce, A.T. Mahan was able to expand to clarify the lectures he prepared in 1885 into *The Influence of Sea Power upon History, 1660-1783* published in 1890.

---

[37] Richard West, *Admirals of American Empire*, (Indianapolis, IN: Bobbs-Merrill Company, 1948), 89, 90.

[38] Zimmermann, *First Great Triumph*, 112.

[39] William Livezey, *Mahan on Sea Power*, (Norman, OK: University of Oklahoma Press, 1981), 12.

[40] Zimmermann, *First Great Triumph*, 92.

Within this book, A.T. Mahan presented a theory for sea power. The theory borrowed heavily from Jomini in both its organization and purpose. The use of principles and their correct application is the methodology that A.T. Mahan used to lay out the theory, which addressed the significance of sea power in the rise and fall of nations. According to Mahan, nations with large commercial and military navies are successful powerful nations. These nations focus on commerce through sea trade. Their sea based commerce and sea lines of communication must be protected by a large offensive, professional navy able to defeat another nation's navy in a decisive battle, and have a sufficient reserves and infrastructure to rapidly refit as the result of loss of a fleet in fleet battle. This fleet must have a way to sustain itself through ports and coaling stations around the globe. The conditions of being a sea power are captured in Mahan's six principles, geographical position, physical conformation, extent of territory, number of population, national character, and character of the government. The writer focuses primarily on the seafaring history of England as an example of a nation that has correctly applied the six principles of sea power. Though this book is presented as a history, it refers frequently to the United States of 1890. Through the explanation of the six principles, it informs a path the United States could take in regards to naval policy.[41]

This theory found purchase in the United States government because it was supportive of American politicians' expansionist views of foreign policy, McDougall defined this period as progressive imperialism, 1898-1917, which focused on protecting the United States and interests by securing naval bases across the world. The United States stopped expanding once these bases were secured and the navy

---

[41] A.T. Mahan, *The Influence of Sea Power,* The key principles define what attributes a nation requires to be a sea power. I. Geographical Position: A country must be situated that it is neither forced to defend itself by land nor induced to seek extension of its territory by way of land, it has, by the very unity of aim directed upon the sea. II. Physical Conformation: A country must have coastline to the sea that has deepwater ports it must seen as a frontier and settled early in the country's history. III. Extent of Territory: The greater the coastline and more ports the greater the sea power potential of a nation. IV. Number of Population: The number of people in the coastal areas available for sea duty. V. National Character: A nation that desires peaceful and extensive commerce. VI. Character of the Government: The government supports the growth a large commercial and military fleet. For more information on each principle of sea power they are explained respectively, 82, 88, 96, 98, 103,112.

was supported globally. The ideas of progressivism took hold in these territories; Americans would go to these places to teach the native inhabitants, the American way to give them a better life.[42] This view of simply expanding to protect the United States and then going to these newly acquired territories and teaching them the American way of is a very altruistic view of expansion. The expansion into the Pacific and then Asia was not just for security but also for increased commerce, prestige, access to markets, etc. Mahan's principles of sea power support this type of expansion and fully embrace the Hamiltonian view of the role of commerce in foreign policy.

A.T. Mahan's theory became the policy of the United States in actions and deeds. His role in the movement of theory to policy was through access to a patron, Theodore Roosevelt, the support of mentor Admiral Stephen Luce, and the broad compatibility of his theory with views of foreign policy. From his position as the president of the Naval War College, and later as a retired officer and renowned theorist, he was able to leverage the support of both his mentor and patron. Admiral Luce publicly proclaimed Mahan as the Jomini for naval operations and this statement cemented his reputation as a theorist.[43] As Theodore Roosevelt continued his political climb culminating with the Presidency, Mahan maintained a relationship with him through correspondence. The ability to access the President in and of itself provided Mahan political capital to influence policy decisions. These factors coupled with a lack of competing interests, from businesses and thinks tanks and other stakeholders ensured a relatively easy transition from theory to policy.

## Billy Mitchell

Billy Mitchell was the son of a United States Senator from a prominent Wisconsin family. At the age of 18, Billy Mitchell left college to join the Army to fight in the Spanish-American War. While

---

[42] McDougall, *Promised Land,* 5.

[43] Livezey, *Mahan on Sea,* 44.

25

serving in that war, then Private Billy Mitchell was identified by General Adolphus Greely as future officer material. At that time, he sent Mitchell to Washington D.C. to receive his commission in the Signal Corps, of which General Greely was the chief. From this point on, General Greely served as a mentor to Billy Mitchell and was deeply involved in managing his career by providing opportunities for professional advancement, whether through promotions, duty positions, and most importantly, exposing him to the airplane as a military tool.[44]

During the Spanish-American War, Mitchell served in Cuba and then transferred to the Philippines. Prior to his arrival, he read all books he could find about the Philippines; upon his arrival, he wrote extensive reports about what he saw. This voluminous writing became a trademark of his later life. Following service in Philippines, he took a year off, 1900 – 1901, to travel through Asia and visit with his family in France. Upon his return, he served in Alaska and Fort Leavenworth, returning to Asia from 1909 to 1912. While there, he took a two-year sabbatical from the Signal Corps to travel, study, and write about the countries of Asia. He then returned stateside and was appointed the General Staff of the Army.[45]

With this appointment, Mitchell became consumed with studying the air operations of the European nations in World War I. In 1916, he was appointed as the temporary chief of the Army aviation section, subsequently paying for his own flying lessons to earn his aviation wings. Mitchell was then sent to Europe to observe and report on allied air operations. Soon after his arrival, the United States entered the war and with Billy Mitchell already positioned in Europe, he served in the aviation section of the Army Expeditionary Force.[46]

---

[44] Roger Burlingame, *General Billy Mitchell Champion of Air Defense*, (New York, NY: McGraw-Hill Book Company, 1952), 26.

[45] Ibid., 60.

[46] Cooke, *Billy Mitchell*, 58.

Following World War I, he returned to the aviation section of the Army staff where he maintained his Brigadier General rank and served as the section's deputy. From this point on, his career became one of the crusaders for air power in the United States, culminating with his Courts-Martial in 1925. Regardless of all the drama and flair that surround him, he produced a theory for air power, presented in pieces, across numerous published works which was later consolidated in his book *Winged Defense*. It advocated the need for the United States government to establish a separate branch of service, an Air Force, to maximize the potential of air power. He defined air power as simply the ability to do things in the air, whether civilian transport or bombing missions. Air power, to him, was the dominant factor in the future development of the world and warfare. He defined aviators as a separate and distinct group with their own culture and values. Billy Mitchell saw that the United States was uniquely positioned, following World War I, to be a world leader in air power due to its economic strength and industrial base. Air, as an environment, was seen as a future battleground that must be competed for and won by one Air Force defeating another. Once air superiority was established, that nation was all but assured of victory; it could bypass the fielded forces and attack the nation's industrial base or population centers. It was believed attacks in such areas would force a nation to surrender do to a loss of will or ability to produce war material.

This concept was based on assumptions that a nations' will to fight can be broken by air power, and that the ability of air power to locate and destroy targets is limitless. [47] Mitchell's combat experience of leading air-ground operations in World War I helped shape these belief as well as his observations of Hugh Trenchard's leadership of the British Royal Air Force.[48] Mitchell based his belief of the future

---

[47] Billy Mitchell, "Winged Defense." In *Roots,* 476.

[48] David Mets, *The Air Campaign John Warden and the Classical Airpower Theorists,* (Maxwell Air Force Base, AL: Air University Press, 1999), Hugh Trenchard was commander of the British Air Force in World War I and he became the Chief of the Air Staff for the Royal Air Force following the war. He was the British version of Billy Mitchell, a dedicated advocate for airpower. Many of his views about the purpose and organization of an air

dominance of airpower on what happened in World War I, primarily the stalemate of trench warfare and its resulting causalities. Using the small sample of air operations in World War I, he observed airplanes breaking through the stalemate and affecting the battlefield, he solidified his beliefs that the air force and aircraft would get bigger, and faster, drop bombs more accurately, and always get through. His views on how the air force should be organized, its role and mission were borrowed almost verbatim from the work of Hugh Trenchard.[49]

This theory was full of practical recommendations about how air power should be organized and employed. It argued that it was a more economical means to defend the United States than was the Navy. Mitchell's argument was based on the simple calculations of the cost of a single battleship versus the number of aircraft that could be purchased with that same amount, the resulting aircrafts' range was compared to the range of a single battleship, and the range of multiple aircraft was greater than that of a single battleship. Using this simple argument, Mitchell deduced that airpower would be a less costly and more effective than the Navy at defending the United States. Beyond these arguments of practice and economics, the belief was that fielded armies and navies could be bypassed and attacks on vital infrastructure would break the morale of its citizens and will of the nation to fight would be lost. This led to policies of strategic bombing of infrastructure as means to accelerate the end of war by directly breaking the morale of the people. Experiences of World War II do not bear this out to be necessarily true.[50]

Billy Mitchell's theory was presented at a time of liberal internationalism in foreign policy. Following World War I, the leader of that school of thought was President Woodrow Wilson. The belief was that the United States must engage with other nations in partnership, especially in the League of

force were adopted by Billy Mitchell. 22. For more information on Hugh Trenchard see David Mets, *The Air Campaign John Warden and the Classical Airpower Theorists* pages 21 to 29.

[49] Ibid., 22.

[50] Mets, *The Air Campaign*, 49, 50.

Nations, to apply the United States' power abroad to shape the outside world's future.[51] Billy Mitchell's theory of air power found little connection to this foreign policy. He argued initially on the grounds of the defense of the United States territory against enemy air threats. Air power was developing in Europe, Asia, and the United States. However, there was not a perceived threat against the homeland following World War I. The ideas of liberal internationalism dictated that the United States faced no perceived threat from Europe and Asia, as the United States foreign policy focused on forming partnerships with other nations.

Billy Mitchell did not have a patron in the government willing to take up his cause per se. Without a specific patron to advance his theory, he engaged the military and political leadership through regular publications and statements to the newspapers. These statements became increasingly more aggressive and inflammatory, culminating with his Courts-Martial in 1925. Another factor beyond Mitchell's controversial persona was that the development and use of air power in the United States was already the subject of regular debate among Congress and military leaders. Billy Mitchell was not unique in his desire to improve the standing of the air power in the United States.[52] This lack of uniqueness meant that he could be cast as merely another advocate for air power rather than a military theorist attempting to influence policy.

## Arthur Cebrowski

Arthur Cebrowski is unique in this group of American military theorists in that his theory is the least mature of the three. Its first public presentation, with co-author John J. Garstka, in the 1998 Naval Proceedings article *"Network-centric Warfare: Its Origin and Future."*[53] In 2005, Arthur Cebrowski

---

[51] McDougall, *Promised Land,* 5.

[52] Phillip Meilinger, "Billy Mitchell." *American Airpower Biography: A Survey of the Field,* http://www.airpower maxwell.af mil/airchronicles/cc/mitch.html (accessed December 26, 2009)

[53] Arthur Cebrowski and John J. Garstka, "Network –Centric Warfare: Its Origin and Future," *Proceedings 124* (January 1998): 28.

passed away from cancer. Cebrowski's passing resulted in his theory never being compiled into a single comprehensive document. It existed in speeches, power point slides, congressional testimony and personal conversations. An attempt to collate this information was belatedly made by James R. Blaker, an associate of Cebrowski in the Department of Defense.

Mr. Blaker met with Cebrowski regularly from 2001 until his death in 2005. Through these sessions, and with Cebrowski's support the content of these meetings were made into a book, *Transforming Military Force: The Legacy of Arthur Cebrowski and Network Centric Warfare.*[54] This book is part personal tribute to the work of Arthur Cebrowski and part explanation of the theorist's thoughts on Network-centric Warfare, military transformation, and the military's role in world affairs. Though the body of work concerning Arthur Cebrowski and Network-centric Warfare theory is considerably smaller than A.T. Mahan and Billy Mitchell, enough exists to determine Cebrowski's patrons and the national interests his theory supported.

Arthur Cebrowski was born in Passaic, New Jersey and was raised and schooled in Hasbrouck Heights, New Jersey. He graduated from Villanova University in 1964, received a commission as an ensign through Naval Reserve Officers Training Corps (NROTC), and went on to serve over 37 years as a naval aviator and command at highest levels of the Navy.

Prior to graduation from Villanova, then Midshipmen Cebrowski was identified by Admiral Hyman Rickover as a candidate for nuclear service because of his high performance in mathematics and science, an opportunity that Cebrowski declined.[55] He continued to excel in mathematics and science receiving his Masters Degree in Computer Systems Management from the Naval Post Graduate School in 1972. From 1980-1981, Cebrowski attended the inaugural class of the Strategic Studies Group (SSG) at

---

[54] Blaker, *Transforming Military Force*, xi.

[55] Ibid., 6. Admiral Hyman Rickover, was known as the "Father of the Nuclear Navy" his was the central figure in the Navy's development of nuclear vessels, which over sixty years of active service he was one of the most influential Admirals in the history of the Navy.

the Naval War College. The SSG is a yearlong program for six to eight Navy, Marine, Air Force, and Coast Guard officers to generate revolutionary naval warfare concepts.[56] While at SSG, he worked with other future Navy flag officers that would play the role of his mentor within the military as he pushed he ideas forward.[57]

Finally, Cebrowski served in several positions that provided access to highest levels of military bureaucracy, at the director level of the Navy and Joint Staff, and upon retirement as the Director of the Office of Force Transformation, Department of Defense, 2001-2005.[58] These experiences at the highest levels of bureaucracy shaped how the theory was implemented. Cebrowski first gained corporate buy-in by using a collaborative approach with key stakeholders within the Department of Defense.

Cebrowski, like Billy Mitchell, saw the promise of technology in future war. From this belief, he spent the rest of his career working on addressing the structural, organizational, and cultural barriers within the military that prevented the bringing of technical promise to fruition.[59] In the 1970's, Cebrowski became interested in the potential of large-scale integrated circuits – computer chips and transistors. The power of large-scale circuitry, self-synchronization and the overall belief in technology became the foundations for Cebrowski in the development of the theory of Network-centric Warfare. This theory gained acceptance and took hold in the military because Cebrowski had a military mentor to assist him and a patron within the government willing to advance the theory to become policy.

---

[56] U.S. Naval War College, "Chief of Naval Operations Strategic Studies Group." U.S. Naval War College, http://www.usnwc.edu/About/Chief-Naval-Operations-Strategic-Studies-Group.aspx (accessed November 15, 2009)

[57] Blaker, *Transforming Military Force*, 10.

[58] Obituary of Arthur Cebrowski, *Washington Post*, November 15, 2005, national edition.

[59] Blaker, *Transforming Military Force*, 9.

As defined, the theory addresses warfare as it moves from the Industrial Age to the Information Age.[60] As the world enters into the Information Age, society's method for creating power and wealth has shifted. Those societies who gain wealth and power do so through their ability to rapidly access and disseminate information. For a military to operate in the Information Age, it too must gain information superiority to use precision violence to defeat opposing forces. The means to gain information superiority and use precision violence is through Network-centric Warfare; the network is the actual information technology. The term, "to network," is the use of the information technology for action. A robustly networked force will dramatically increase combat power. Thus, United States armed forces are required to have new technology, new operational concepts, and new structures. In the Information Age, United States armed forces will be dispersed, Joint, smaller, more agile, and will mass effects instead of massing actual forces. The forces will be able to do this because of a near-perfect shared view of the environment.

Moving chronologically, Cebrowski found his first key patron in his 1980-1981 class of the Strategic Studies Group (SSG) at the Naval War College. During that course, he was a student with fellow Navy Commander, Bill Owens. Cebrowski and Owens formed a friendship based on shared perspective of three components: (1) change in military affairs was essential, (2) it was not going to come easily, and (3) because of the first two points, the logic for changing had to be solid and articulation relentless.[61]

---

[60] David S. Alberts, Daniel S. Papp, *The Information Age: An Anthology on Its Impact and Consequences,* eds. David S. Alberts, Daniel S. Papp (Washington, DC: Command and Control Research Program, 2007), 2. http://www.dodccrp.org/files/Alberts_Anthology_I.pdf Accessed (February 7, 2010) The Information Age is the concluding years of the twentieth century and the beginning of the twenty-first century. This characterization of our time is based on the widespread proliferation of emerging information and communication technologies and the capabilities that those technologies provide and will provide humankind to overcome the barriers imposed on communications by time, distance, and location and the limits and constraints inherent in human capacities to process information and make decisions. The Industrial Age is understood to be the period prior to the Information Age.

[61] Blaker, *Transforming Military Force,* 11.

In 1996, Cebrowski served as Director, Command, Control, Communications and Computers (J-6), Joint Staff. His friend from Naval War College, Bill Owens, was then serving as the Vice Chairman of the Joint Staff. These two friends worked together and contributed to the Joint Staff document *Joint Vision 2010*.[62] The *Joint Vision 2010* was billed by the Chairman of the Joint Chiefs of Staff General John Shalikashvili as a "template for future U.S. military operations."[63] This initiative did not continue to grow after the normal change out of military personnel.

Secretary of Defense Donald Rumsfeld arrived at the Pentagon with the force of the 2000 Bush-Cheney campaign pledge to the military that "help is on the way."[64] With this mandate for change in the air, Secretary Rumsfeld appointed Arthur Cebrowski to serve as the director of the newly-created Office of Force Transformation. From this position, Cebrowski was able to take up the work he began in *Joint Vision 2010*. Cebrowski served in this position from 2001 until his death in 2005. During that time, he worked closely with Secretary Rumsfeld to advance the concepts of transformation and Network-centric Warfare. In Secretary Rumsfeld, Cebrowski found someone who believed in the concepts of Network-centric Warfare and was willing to support Cebrowski's own initiatives.

Given this broad support from such a prominent patron in the government, Cebrowski's theory of Network-centric Warfare was introduced and received support throughout the military. With Cebrowski's death in 2005 and the subsequent departure of Secretary Rumsfeld, the future of Network-centric Warfare is in doubt. In 2006, the Office of Force Transformation was closed and its duties and

---

[62] *Joint Vision 2010* (Washington, DC: Joint Staff, 1996), 1. This vision of future warfighting embodies the improved intelligence and command and control available in the information age and goes on to develop four operational concepts: dominant maneuver, precision engagement, full dimensional protection, and focused logistics.

[63] Blaker, *Transforming Military Force*, 14.

[64] Ibid., 22.

responsibilities moved to other organizations in the Pentagon.[65] The benefit of information technology to link widely-dispersed forces on the battlefield has been proven successful through the combat experiences of both, Afghanistan and Iraq. The Navy continues to position itself as the service leader in the use of the network and information to enable combat operations.[66] The Navy is not, however, actively pursuing Network-centric Warfare as a theory of war rather than as a concept for future naval operations. If Network-centric Warfare theory is to continue development as a feasible military theory for the United States government, it must find both a new intellectual leader to continue to develop the theory and a willing patron to advance the theory to become policy.

Arthur Cebrowski's theory was not initially developed with an eye towards the broader issues of foreign policy. However, it did find some connection with the foreign policy tradition of the time, global meliorism, a tradition that dictated that United States position as world hegemon following the Cold War should be used to improve other countries.[67] He was able to see the value of Network-centric Warfare theory only by using Barnett's concept "functioning core" and "non-integrated gap" worldview. Cebrowski considered the U.S. military as a possible vehicle for extending the benefits of globalization to those of the non-integrated gap.[68] This idea of the United States military operating under Network-centric Warfare theory and aiding in globalization is not fully articulated by Cebrowski. It is not clear if this requires the military to do something globally that only Network-centric Warfare theory can provide the force or if it is the renaming of ongoing military operations. Lacking broad acceptance of the concept of

---

[65] Josh Rogin, "DOD Decides to Close Office of Force Transformation," *Federal Computer Week*, http://fcw.com/articles/2006/09/04/dod-decides-to-close-office-of-force-transformation.aspx accessed (December 13, 2009)

[66] Gary Roughead, "White Paper in the U.S. Navy Information Domination Concept" (U.S. Navy, 2009)

[67] McDougall, *Promised Land,* 198.

[68] Blaker, *Transforming Military Force*, 216.

34

the core and gap states and the process of globalization, Cebrowski's ideas of extending its benefits has not lent it to being a compelling theory for continued adherence.

Arthur Cebrowski did have a military mentor and a patron that supported his efforts, as well as the added benefit of the indirect support of a think tank that informed policymakers. Cebrowski also used a method of informing stakeholders that was based building consensus and buy-in.

# Comparison of Theorists

## Common Military Experiences

The works of A.T. Mahan, Billy Mitchell, and Arthur Cebrowski are a progression of action-focused military theory as developed through the lens of United State foreign policy and the confluence of stakeholders both inside and outside of the government. These three theorists' careers trace similar arcs through the military and political bureaucracies.

They all possess similar credentials that aided in their advancing military theory through these bureaucracies. Senior military leaders identified all three theorists' potential early in their careers. This early identification in and of itself is not decisive but provides, at a minimum, foreshadowing of what was to become of these officers military careers. Admiral Stephen Luce discovered A.T. Mahan during the Civil War. General Adolphus Greely found Billy Mitchell as an eighteen year-old who he soon got a commission as a Lieutenant. Admiral Rickover identified Arthur Cebrowski while still a cadet, but Cebrowski did not pursue nuclear service in the Navy leaving that potential relationship unformed. In the cases of A.T Mahan and Billy Mitchell, those senior leaders who indentified them served as mentors to these budding military theorists. Cebrowski did not have Admiral Rickover as a mentor but that officer was not the only senior leader see the potential of Cebrowski. As previously noted, Admiral Bill Owens, a classmate of Cebrowski's, served as a mentor while they were both working at the Pentagon.

All three theorists became flag officers. By achieving the rank of general officer, the theorists were able to serve in or have access to the highest levels of the military, where theory intersects with

35

policy. This placement allowed for access to the key stakeholders within and around the government. A.T. Mahan is the exception to this in that his promotion to Rear Admiral came after his retirement. Regardless of that, A.T. Mahan's rank of Captain carried the same weight, as a flag officer, as both in Mitchell and Cebrowski's times. He was able to access the highest levels of the Navy and the government through his position as President of the Naval War College and through the exposure of his writings. Mahan's work was disseminated widely through key stakeholders through the advocacy of Theodore Roosevelt.

All three theorists were combat veterans. These combat experiences ranged from modest to revolutionary. A.T. Mahan rode out blockade duty during the Civil War. Arthur Cebrowski flew over one-hundred and fifty combat missions in Vietnam. [69] Billy Mitchell commanded the air phase of the Battle of Saint-Mihiel, one of the first coordinated air-ground offensives in history. [70] Regardless of the scale of their individual combat experience, it shaped their futures and the theories they developed and advanced.

In the case of A.T. Mahan, he described his experience during the Civil War as excessively dry bones, woeful material of remembered incidents. [71] Accordingly, his experience did not directly contribute to the development of his theory, the monotony of this service, however, did shape his future career path. Some biographers state that Mahan did not like either the Navy or the tedium of ship duty interrupting his preferred shore duty. Reinforcing this view is Mahan seeking special consideration to avoid sea duty to continue writing in his capacity as President of the Naval War College. [72] However,

---

[69] Obituary of Arthur Cebrowski, *Washington Post*, November 15, 2005, national edition.

[70] Meilinger, "Billy Mitchell." *American Airpower.*

[71] A.T. Mahan, *From Sail to Steam*, (New York, NY: Harper & Brothers, 1907), 188.

[72] Ibid., 311. For more information on an assessment A.T. Mahan's Navy career see also; Richard West, *Admirals of American Empire*, (Indianapolis, IN: Bobbs-Merrill Company, 1948); William Livezey, *Mahan on Sea Power*, (Norman, OK: University of Oklahoma Press, 1981).

36

A.T. Mahan was not a passionate or exceptional sea-going officer, he was capable and professional when at sea. His passion and ultimately his contributions lay on shore not at sea.

Billy Mitchell's experience in combat, culminating with command of combined air forces in a coordinated air-ground attack in World War I solidified his view of the future dominance of airpower in the future. This effort, along with the relationships, he formed with British and French aviators, particularly British Major General Hugh Trenchard, became instrumental in Mitchell's work. The knowledge Mitchell gained about air operations from Trenchard provided a base for Mitchell's theory of air power.[73]

Arthur Cebrowski's combat experience was formative in the development of the theory of Network-centric Warfare. Cebrowski saw the introduction of large-scale integrated circuits in aircraft as a means to allow the pilot to focus less on the actual mechanics of flying and targeting and more time on maneuver and defeating the enemy. This technology would have dramatically changed Cebrowski's combat experience and, from this noted deficiency; Cebrowski pursued a theory that focused on technology as means to increase combat effectiveness at the individual level.

## The Role of Technology in Theory

Technology is a component that shows the contrast of the scope of the theories over time. Mitchell and Cebrowski developed theories that required assumptions about technology to underpin their theory. This focus on technology narrows the scope of the theory because it cannot adequately address developments of technology that affect their underpinning technology. As previously discussed, Billy Mitchell's air power theory found limited success in World War II, when assumptions about the effectiveness of bomber aircraft to reach their targets was countered by the new technology and increased effectiveness of anti-aircraft guns.

---

[73] Burlingame, *General Billy Mitchell*, 66, 67.

All three advocated for the creation of a military force based on the capabilities of current and emerging technology. Mahan's theory did not make explicit assumptions about technology in his theory, whereas, Cebrowski and Mitchell made decisions based on the perceived potential of emerging technology. To A.T. Mahan a surface fleet that could defeat an enemy fleet in decisive battle was paramount, emerging technologies like submarine, torpedoes, and aircraft carrier would cause changes in tactics not the principles of his theory of sea power and the preeminence of the surface fleet.[74] This concept holds true so long as the technology of the surface fleet can defeat the technology of submarines, torpedoes, and any other emerging sea-based weapons, which to date is the case.

Billy Mitchell saw aircraft as the future of warfare. This concept used the assumption that, aeronautical technology would continue to improve at a rate greater than the technology of armies and navies. To Mitchell, the aircraft technological advantage over ground and sea forces was a permanent condition preventing nations from ever developing a means to defend against air power.[75] The idea that the bomber would always get through was resident in not just Mitchell's work, but also in the work of other air power theorists like Giulio Douhet.[76]

Arthur Cebrowski's theory states that the nature of war is unchanging but that war in the Information Age would be fought in a different competitive space.[77] Though Cebrowski argued for organizational and cultural changes within the Department of Defense, his focus was on the development and implementation of information technology. Again, like Billy Mitchell, Cebrowski saw information

---

[74] Livezey, *Mahan on Sea Power*, 315.

[75] Mitchell, "Winged Defense." In *Roots,* 439.

[76] Mets, *The Air Campaign*, Giulio Douhet was an Italian Army officer who commanded Italy's first aviation battalion before World War I. He was prolific writer and air power theorist, with the tenets of the offensive nature of airpower and the belief that the bomber would always get through. These concepts were also seen in the work of Hugh Trenchard and Billy Mitchell. 12, 22. For more information on Giulio Douhet see David Mets, *The Air Campaign John Warden and the Classical Airpower Theorists* pages 11 to 18.

[77] Office of Force Transformation, *The Implementation of Network,* summary of major themes of The Implementation of the Network-centric Warfare.

technology as developing at a rate that would exceed the rate of opponents to the system. The network in Cebrowski's view would be able to counter all threats and remain connected regardless of enemy activity.

Technology, and its ability to deliver the promises, remains paramount for the theories to retain their prominence. The problem for Mitchell is what happens when the bomber cannot always get through because of a ground or sea based anti-aircraft threat? How does Cebrowski counter a threat that can enter the network? Once technology fails to deliver on its promises, these theories lose some of their luster. They must fall back on the principles of the theory; this gives the theory its flexibility to meet with the changes of technology. Mahan's theory of sea power has been an enduring globally-accepted theory with principles that have become firmly entrenched in military theory. Mahan's work has been resilient to the challenges that technology has presented. Billy Mitchell's theory of air power has some principles that remain, such as air superiority, destroying the enemy air force on the ground, attacking strategic targets. Where technology trumped the theory was in the assumption that land and sea forces would be unable to defeat an air threat. Technology exists that can defend land and sea forces from an air threat and limit their ability to attack strategic targets like population and manufacturing centers.

Cebrowski's theory has seen its greatest challenge in modern conflicts in which the United States currently finds itself. Iraq and Afghanistan have shown the limits of technology to provide timely accurate information in a counterinsurgency environment. Using fewer troops with more technology does not meet the requirements of an effective counterinsurgency campaign, and its requirement for personal relationships among the population. Technology as a basis of a military theory, like those found in the ideas of Mitchell and Cebrowski, are less durable to unforeseen changes in technology. Mitchell and Cebrowski's theories faced resistance by those who observed the current technology and saw that it was not able to realize fully the view of the theorist. As long as airplanes crashed at an alarming rate, Mitchell's theory could be resisted; as long as there was a lack bandwidth to support Cebrowski's Information Technology, his theory will to face resistance.

39

Mahan's principles, like Jomini's, can find applicability across history. To apply their theory, Mitchell and Cebrowski require certain technologies; this reliance on technology creates theories that are sensitive to any major technological changes. Beyond these questions of durability and technology, all three theories place at the center the protection of the United States and its interests.

## Theory's Support of Foreign Policy

As discussed within the case studies the theories of Mahan, Mitchell, and Cebrowski all provide support to the national interests as defined by the foreign policy traditions and schools of thought of their time. The evolution of the theories trends towards the idea of doing more with less. In the case of war, the theories of Mitchell and Cebrowski shift towards bringing a swift end to conflict, minimizing noncombatant casualties and wanton destruction of another nation.

Billy Mitchell directly attacked the cost of maintaining a large fleet of capital ships to protect the United States and its interests. He argued that aircraft were cheaper and, in most cases, more efficient and effective in meeting the tasks of national security in the emerging post World War I world. Arthur Cebrowski argued along a similar line, that investing in advanced information technology rather than more combat platforms leads to more efficient, effective, and less expensive force. A non-networked force must physically mass forces to achieve effects with non-precision guided munitions. A networked force does not have to mass forces to achieve effects; they rely on shared information across distance and achieve mass by using precision guided munitions.

Billy Mitchell understood firsthand the horrors of trench warfare in World War I and thus had a strong desire to prevent another such massacre from occurring again. The airplane, he argued, could provide a quicker, more decisive victory than was seen in the stalemate of World War I. The more humane victory would come in the form of bombing both population and manufacturing centers to break the will of the people. Ideally, he reasoned that nations would be more reluctant to go to war knowing that their opponent had an air force capable of reaching their population and manufacturing centers. The risks of this destruction would, therefore, outweigh the benefits of the war.[78]

Arthur Cebrowski's theory also identified technology as means to make war quicker and more decisive. Through near-perfect intelligence and surveillance technology, networked to the operating force using precision-guided weapons, allows for reduced destruction and loss of life, all while having a smaller footprint on the modern battlefield. The theory allows the United States military to bring destruction of only the enemy while sparing the infrastructure of the enemy nation and its noncombatants. Network-centric Warfare theory defines this ability as the precise application of force that achieves precision effects.[79] To successfully advocate for a military theory it must be compatible with the foreign policy goals of the nation. If the theory does not align with the foreign policy, it will be handicapped throughout the process, as was the case with Billy Mitchell. Regardless, of alignment with policy a theorist must advocate for their theory in a way that is effective and consistent with military ethics. The way in which the theorist, developed their theory and later advocated for it, is not only linked to military ethics but their education as well.

## Theorists' Education

The educational experiences of the three theorists shaped how they developed their theories and later advocated for them. All three theorists relied on self-study and a depth of intellectual curiosity to develop the foundation from which they built their theories. As previously presented in theorists's section, their educational experiences are noteworthy. However, there are differences among the three, most prominently the more informal education of A.T. Mahan and Billy Mitchell in contrast to the formal education of Arthur Cebrowski.

---

[78] Mitchell, "Winged Defense." In *Roots,* 441.

[79] Office of Force Transformation, *The Implementation of Network,* 23.

A.T. Mahan was a graduate of Annapolis and that was his last foray into formal education. Billy Mitchell left college to fight in the Spanish American War. Arthur Cebrowski graduated from Villanova and then at the appropriate point in his career he went to the Naval Post Graduate School. A.T. Mahan and Billy Mitchell's careers are rife with sabbaticals, travel and interesting jobs. These broad experiences and the education they provided stand in stark contrast to the career of Cebrowski. His performance as a naval officer is exceptional by virtue of rank achieved and positions held. Nevertheless, the current system, which Cebrowski served under, produces generals and does little to reward creativity and moral courage. Officers rise to flag rank by following remarkably similar career patterns. Senior generals, both active and retired, are the most important figures in determining an officer's potential for flag rank.[80]

Regardless of the differences in the types of education they received, their remains one thing that binds these theorists education, that is, they all developed their theories through self-study and personal intellectual curiosity. They were directed by neither a mentor or a patron to develop a specific theory nor were they formally educated in the methods of theory development, advocacy, and application. Through their education, whether formal or informal and personal experiences these three officers developed a theory that they then advocated for to shape United States policy.

## Methods of Advocacy

The image of A.T. Mahan and Billy Mitchell as theorists and officers is far more provocative than the rather staid image of Arthur Cebrowski. Mahan and Mitchell were controversial figures throughout their careers. In 1893, A.T. Mahan had Teddy Roosevelt intervene to protect his career from a rather damning fitness report from Rear Admiral Henry Erben for his service on the U.S.S Chicago.[81] Billy

---

[80] Paul Yingling, "A Failure in Generalship," *Armed Forces Journal*, (May, 2007), http://www.armedforcesjournal.com/2007/05/2635198 (accessed January 5, 2010)

[81] Richard Turk, *The Ambiguous Relationship Theodore Roosevelt and Alfred Thayer Mahan*, (New York, NY: Greenwood Press, 1987), 18.

Mitchell was convicted in a 1925 Courts-Martial for insubordination. These are just two examples of where A.T. Mahan and Billy Mitchell have stepped out line with their peers and superiors to advance their theory. No such controversy follows Arthur Cebrowski. This does not to imply that in order to be a successful military theorist one must be controversial, rather, it shows that the conditions within the military have changed dramatically from the times of A.T. Mahan and Billy Mitchell. The military and the government at-large have become more professional, more bureaucratic, more specialized, and subject to more influences. These changes determine the methods of advocacy a theorist must use.

Another way A.T. Mahan and Billy Mitchell stepped out of line is in the manner each theorist chose to advocate his theory and to what audience they chose to engage. A.T. Mahan was a prolific writer with over ten books and over one hundred articles to his credit. These books and articles were broadly available to the public and found throughout prominent periodicals of the time. Billy Mitchell followed a similar approach as A.T. Mahan; he authored nine books and had over one hundred articles to his credit, and was always willing to provide a reporter a quote for the newspaper. This engagement of the public in military theory, and eventual policy debate, was an approach not pursued by Arthur Cebrowski. He intentionally wrote little about his theory, relying more on speeches and power point slides to lead a discussion about his ideas and make them accessible for input and revision. He was seeking synthesis of his ideas with others to improve the theory.[82] These two distinct approaches show the evolution of professionalism and specialization in the United States government. Writing for profit while still serving on active duty is neither generally considered the conduct of a professional officer nor is likely to be an effective tool to gain collaboration with the other stakeholders.

---

[82] Issac Don Levine, *Mitchell Pioneer of Air Power*, (New York, NY: Duell, Sloan and Pearce, 1942), 401, Livezey, *Mahan on Sea Power,* 387, Blaker, *Transforming Military Force*, 202.

# Conclusion

The careers of A.T Mahan, Billy Mitchell, and Arthur Cebrowski stretch from the Civil War to the ongoing wars in Iraq and Afghanistan. The three theorists by no means provide an indelible line traceable back through one hundred forty years of military theory development. This line is, rather, one that evolves with the conditions of the military, government and American public. There is an informal process by which a military officer can advance theory through the government to create policy. By understanding this process, policymakers and military professionals alike can better identify a military theorist and assist how he/she, can advance a theory to policy.

A military theorist does not receive formal training or education to be a theorist; they are products of their own self-study and experiences, and are discovered and mentored by a senior military officer. The theorist must also have the active support of a patron in the government. The theorist must be governed by sound military ethics while operating at the policy level of government. The needs of the Nation trump the needs of the theory or theorist. The theory must be attuned to national interests and the current foreign policy environment. The military theorist must be a senior officer with a military patron that supports their work, and can advocate and guide them as necessary. The theorist must also have the placement and access necessary to advance their theory through the appropriate patron in the government. A.T. Mahan was the President of the Naval War College, Mitchell and Cebrowski both worked at the general staff level in their respective service. All three theorists had a military mentor at crucial points in their careers who enabled the theorist to advance his theory. They also had patron in the government that took up their cause.

The military theory must have a purpose that clearly contributes to the preservation of the United States and furthers its goals. Mahan and Mitchell's theory of sea power and air power respectively, protect the homeland; Cebrowski's theory could support expanding the benefits of globalization to other nations. The theory must be able to address the challenges of balancing the elements of Clausewitz's trinity while simultaneously providing the framework for action that Jomini provides. The theorist must

44

construct the theory broadly enough to attune it to the current climate of foreign policy. This balancing is resident in Cebrowski's theory with its links to key stakeholders, such as the *Project for a New American Century*.

The officer, if he/she is to influence the advancement of the theory, must be educated in the intricacies of the bureaucracies and the making of policy in the government. This is an informal education gained by working at the upper echelons of the military and government and a mentor is present in all three theorists' biographies. Currently, this type of education focuses on developing the ability to collaborate with many stakeholders and gain support from them within the limits of military ethics. A formal military education of how to determine policy is outside the scope a professional officer.

The officer is competing with various stakeholders for the attention of policymakers and patrons in the government. These stakeholders reside primarily in the areas of think tanks and the defense industry. These stakeholders also have more longevity in the government and have a broader network of associates in and around the government. To compete against the evolving challenge of increased stakeholders, the military theorist must remained engaged with the government policymakers far beyond the normal military assignment of two to three years. All three theorists were able to remain engaged in the process for an extended period. A.T. Mahan retired from the Navy and continued to write on the subject of sea power and foreign policy; Mitchell also continued to publish to advocate for air power. Upon Cebrowski's retirement, he became a civilian director in the Department of Defense to continue his efforts in Network-centric warfare. Actually, all three theorist were still engaged with their theory and the government up until the time of their death.

Another subtle point, these three theorists were never trained, groomed, or asked by someone in the government or the military to develop a theory. It was through self-study that these officers developed their theories. If this condition is to define the nature by which military officers become theorists, then it becomes incumbent on the potential mentor to identify the military officers with the necessary predilection to be a theorist. This also speaks to the rarity in which military theorists are found

45

and developed within the military. It becomes a meeting of ability and chance, if both civilian and military leaders do not recognize the other factors that affect the process by a military theory becomes policy.

These points are not a checklist to ensure success for the burgeoning military theorist, rather, they are points of continuity and risk that must be understood to compete in the environment that comprises today's United States government bureaucracy. Understanding these points, and how they play on both the development and implementation of military theory into policy, is a key understanding required for all potential theorists and policy-makers. Only through this understanding of the confluence of stakeholders-interests, national policy, and military capability-can those on the path less travelled, that of a military officer developing and advocating theory; ensure a proper and beneficial role in determining the nation's future course.